A Guide for Using

Johnny Tremain

in the Classroom

Based on the novel written by Esther Forbes

This guide written by John Lockett Haack
Illustrated by Keith Vasconcelles

Teacher Created Resources, Inc.
6421 Industry Way
Westminster, CA 92683
www.teachercreated.com
©1994 Teacher Created Resources, Inc.
Reprinted, 2005
Made in U.S.A.
ISBN 1-55734-440-X

Table of Contents

Introduction 3

Sample Lesson Plan 4

Before the Book *(Pre-reading Activities)* 5

About the Author 6

Book Summary 7

Vocabulary Lists 8

Vocabulary Activity Ideas 9

Section 1 *(Chapter I through III)* 10
- ❏ Quiz Time!
- ❏ Hands-on Project—*Stamp of Approval*
- ❏ Cooperative Learning Activity—*We Can Work It Out*
- ❏ Curriculum Connections—*Health: First Aid*
- ❏ Into Your Life—*Reading Response Journals*

Section 2 *(Chapters IV and V)* 15
- ❏ Quiz Time!
- ❏ Hands-on Project—*Have Your Cake and Eat It Too!*
- ❏ Cooperative Learning Activity—*You Be the Judge*
- ❏ Curriculum Connections—*Math: Around a Pound*
- ❏ Into Your Life—*An Heirloom, I Presume*

Section 3 *(Chapters VI and VII)* 20
- ❏ Quiz Time!
- ❏ Hands-on Project—*Quill Skill*
- ❏ Cooperative Learning Activity—*Masquerade Model*
- ❏ Curriculum Connections—*Social Studies. Tea For You?*
- ❏ Into Your Life—*Some Facts About Tax*

Section 4 *(Chapters VIII through X)* 25
- ❏ Quiz Time!
- ❏ Hands-on Project—*Tin Can Lantern*
- ❏ Cooperative Learning Activity—*The Famous Ride*
- ❏ Curriculum Connections—*Geography: Mapping Out Revere's Ride*
- ❏ Into Your Life—*Charting Your Family Tree*

Section 5 *(Chapters XI through XII)* 33
- ❏ Quiz Time!
- ❏ Hands-on Project—*Light the Night!*
- ❏ Cooperative Learning Activity—*Love America*
- ❏ Curriculum Connections—*Language Arts: Keen Observations*
- ❏ Into Your Life—*Uniforms Then and Now*

After the Book *(Post-reading Activities)*

Any Questions? 38

Book Report Ideas 39

Research Ideas 40

Culminating Activity 41

Unit Test Options 43

Bibliography of Related Reading 46

Answer Key 47

Introduction

A good book can touch our lives like a good friend. Within its pages are words and characters that can inspire us to achieve our highest ideals. We can turn to it for companionship, recreation, comfort, and guidance. It can also give us a cherished story to hold in our hearts forever.

In Literature Units, great care has been taken to select books that are sure to become good friends! Teachers who use this unit will find the following features to supplement their own valuable ideas.

- Sample Lesson Plans
- Pre-reading Activities
- A Biographical Sketch and Picture of the Author
- A Book Summary
- Vocabulary Lists and Suggested Vocabulary Activities
- Chapters grouped for study, with each section including:

    – *quizzes*

    – *hands-on projects*

    – *cooperative learning activities*

    – *cross-curriculum connections*

    – *extensions into the reader's own life*

- Post-reading Activities
- Book Report Ideas
- Research Ideas
- A Culminating Activity
- Three Different Options for Unit Tests
- Bibliography
- Answer Key

We are confident that this unit will be a valuable addition to your planning, and we hope your students will increase the circle of friends they have in books!

Sample Lesson Plan

Each of the lessons suggested below takes one or more days to complete.

Lesson 1

- Introduce and have students complete some or all of the pre-reading activities found on page 5.
- Read "About the Author" with your students. (page 6)
- Discuss what it would be like to be without parents or family at the age of four. Discuss ways a young person could earn enough money to support himself.
- Introduce the vocabulary list for Section 1. (page 8)

Lesson 2

- Read Chapters I through III. As you read, place the vocabulary words in the context of the story and discuss their meanings.
- Choose a vocabulary activity. (page 9)
- Make a vegetable print stamp. (page 11)
- Students working in groups play real-life situations in which someone's feelings are hurt. (page 12)
- Discuss the book in terms of health and first aid.
- Begin Reading Response Journals. (page 14)
- Administer the Section 1 quiz. (page 10)
- Introduce the vocabulary list for Section 2. (page 8)

Lesson 3

- Read Chapters IV and V. Place the vocabulary words in context and discuss their meanings.
- Choose a vocabulary activity. (page 9)
- Learn how to make Queen's Cake. (page 16)
- Working in groups, give impromptu speeches. (page 17)
- Discuss the book in terms of British money. (page 18)
- Discuss and write about a treasured heirloom. (page 19)
- Administer Section 2 quiz. (page 15)
- Introduce the vocabulary list for Section 3.

Lesson 4

- Read Chapters VI and VII. Place the vocabulary words in context and discuss their meanings.
- Make quill pens. (page 21)
- Create Native American costumes from recycled newspapers. (page 22)
- Do research to learn about tea. (page 23)
- Learn how taxes affect you and your family. (page 24)

- Administer Section 3 quiz. (page 20)
- Introduce the vocabulary list for Section 4. (page 8)

Lesson 5

- Read Chapters VIII through X. Place vocabulary words in context and discuss their meanings.
- Choose a vocabulary activity. (page 9)
- Make a tinware lantern. (page 26)
- Work together to dramatize "Paul Revere's Ride." (pages 27 - 29)
- Discuss the book in terms of geography and map reading. (pages 30 and 31)
- Become a genealogist and chart your family tree. (pages 32)
- Administer Section 4 quiz. (page 25)
- Introduce the vocabulary list for Section 5. (page 8)

Lesson 6

- Read Chapters XI and XII. Place vocabulary words in context and discuss their meanings.
- Choose a vocabulary activity. (page 9)
- Make a colonial candle. (page 34)
- Work together to generate ways to "Love America!" (page 35)
- Test your observation skills. (page 36)
- Discuss how wearing a uniform can change a person's behavior. Illustrate and write about a favorite uniform. (page 37)
- Administer Section 5 quiz. (page 33)

Lesson 7

- Discuss any questions your students may have about the book. (page 38)
- Assign book report and research projects. (pages 39 and 40)
- Begin work on a culminating activity. (pages 41 and 42)

Lesson 8

- Administer Unit Tests 1, 2, and/or 3. (pages 43-45)
- Discuss the test answers and possibilities.
- Discuss the students' enjoyment of the book.
- Provide a list of related books for your students. (page 46)

Before the Book

Before you begin reading *Johnny Tremain* with your students, do some pre-reading activities to stimulate their interest and enhance comprehension. Below are some activities that might work well in your class.

1. Predict what the story is about based on the book's title.

2. Predict what the story is about based on the cover illustration.

3. Find out if students have ever heard of Esther Forbes and ask them if they know anything about her personal life or her writing.

4. Answer these questions:

   Are you interested in:

   – stories that take place long ago?

   – stories in which a character overcomes a great setback?

   – stories of excitement and danger?

   – stories about famous Americans?

   Would you:

   – be content to work six days a week and twelve hours a day?

   – learn to write neatly with your other hand?

   – forgive someone who purposely injured you?

   – risk your life for your country?

   – be able to survive without the help of family members?

   Have you ever been seriously hurt in an accident? Describe your experience.

5. Working in groups or teams, research and report on aspects of colonial life. Choose from such topics as education, clothing, homes, occupations, transportation, and pastimes.

About the Author

Esther Forbes was born on June 28, 1891, in Westborough, Massachusetts. The youngest of five children, she spent her childhood surrounded by books and history. Her spacious home was filled with memorabilia and household goods from early America. Her family owned, for example, a treasured bedspread embroidered by the mother and grandmother of Samuel Adams.

As a young girl, Esther enjoyed reading, and riding her pony through the woods and pastures around nearby Worcester. Sometimes she stopped to collect a new turtle to add to her collection. At one time she had as many as fifty shelled pets!

Esther was educated at the Brancroft School in Worcester, the Brandford Academy in Brandford, and at the University of Wisconsin. While she was at the University, World War I was in progress. Many young men had left their farms to enlist as soldiers and a shortage of farm labor resulted. When students were called on to help, Esther joined in, becoming a hand on a farm near Harper's Ferry, Virginia. Her duties included shucking corn, picking apples, and driving a team of horses.

When the war ended, she joined the editorial staff of Houghton Mifflin. Yet her love for the outdoors remained. She spent several of her vacation periods helping with the harvest near Harper's Ferry.

After six years with Houghton Mifflin, Esther married and did some traveling abroad. Her career as a book author began in 1926 with the instant success of *Oh Genteel Lady.* More books followed, including *Mirror for Witches, The General's Lady,* and *Paul Revere and the World He Lived In.* While working on *Paul Revere and the World He Lived In,* she became interested in the life of apprentices in 18th-century Boston. While doing research for the book, she learned that Paul Revere's father was an apprentice to a goldsmith who had fled France for a better life in America. Esther wrote:

> "Apprenticeship was something of a short-term form of slavery. There was no disgrace to it. It was the only way skilled trades (including medicine) were taught."

Esther Forbes received the Pulitzer Prize for history in 1943 for *Paul Revere and the World He Lived In.* In 1944, her novel, *Johnny Tremain,* won the Newbery Medal. Esther Forbes died in 1967, but her love for history was passed on. At her death she bequeathed the royalties from her works to the American Antiquarian Society of Worcester, Massachusetts, the place where she had done most of the research for her books.

Johnny Tremain

by Esther Forbes
(Dell Publishing Co., 1987)
(Available in Canada, Doubleday Dell Seal; UK, Doubleday Bantam Dell; AUS, Transworld Pub.)

Johnny Tremain, a fourteen-year-old orphan, is an apprentice to silversmith, Mr. Lapham. Johnny is a skilled artisan, and he knows it. If it weren't for Johnny's aid, Lapham's smithshop would surely close down. Because of his skill, Johnny acts as overseer of the workshop, even giving orders to sixteen-year-old Dove, another apprentice boy. Dove is angered by Johnny's haughtiness and jealous of his prestige at the Laphams, so he plays a trick on Johnny which leads to Johnny's having a burned hand. Now useless as a silversmith, Johnny sets out for other work.

However, this proves to be a difficult task since no one wants to hire a boy who is "not whole." Nevertheless, Johnny finally finds work delivering newspapers for the *Boston Observer,* a patriotic newspaper published by Johnny's new found friend Rab and Rab's uncle. The living quarters which Johnny and Rab share are the meeting place of the Observers' Club, a group of politically ambitious Whigs led by none other than Samuel Adams and John Hancock.

Johnny's part-time job performing odds-and-ends tasks at the Afric Queen, a nearby restaurant and local hangout of British officers, affords Johnny the privilege of collecting information to take back to the Whigs. With Johnny's aid, not only do the Sons of Liberty successfully throw all of the imported tea into the Boston Harbor, but some of the information Johnny learns aids the Whigs in planning to assemble the Minute Men as an army. They defeat the British forces in the battles at Lexington and Concord. Johnny learns through observing the death of his friend Rab that the call for liberty, while necessary, is bought at a high price.

Through Johnny's eyes, the reader can understand a portion of the struggles both internal and external which the Colonists felt in the events which led to the American Revolution.

Vocabulary Lists

The vocabulary lists on this page correspond to each sectional grouping of chapters. Vocabulary activity ideas can be found on page 9 of this book.

Section 1
Chapters I-III

alewife	aloof	annealing	apprentice	assuage
belligerent	broadsides	crucible	felon	flaccid
grog	hovels	indolent	maimed	pesthouse
rakish	splayed	venerable	wry	

Section 2
Chapters IV-V

ardent	atrophying	cavorting	discomfiture	fagot
fatuous	genteel	knaves	militia	ruddy
seditious	trussed	turnkey	wary	

Section 3
Chapters VI-VII

brig	demeanor	divulge	gesticulate	henchman
inflammatory	inundated	machinations	parody	paroxysm
sedition	truckle	tyranny	warped	winches

Section 4
Chapters VIII-X

ardor	befuddled	bilious	canny	cupola
defaced	dilatory	enmity	flog	florid
garrulous	grenadier	lassitude	lucid	malice
paunch	piqued	placate	punctilious	queue
rogue	stoically	sullen	swilling	turbulent

Section 5
Chapters XI-XII

animosity	billeted	epaulets	facings	glibly
haggard	huzzaed	protegee	surfeited	tremolo

8

Vocabulary Activity lieas

Help your students learn and retain the vocabulary in *Johnny Tremain* with these vocabulary activities.

- People of all ages like to make and solve puzzles. Ask your students to make their own **Crossword Puzzles** or **Wordsearch Puzzles** using the vocabulary words from the story.

- Challenge your students to a **Vocabulary Bee!** This is similar to a spelling bee, but the game participants must correctly define the words as well as spell them.

- Play **Vocabulary Concentration.** The goal of this game is to match vocabulary words with their definitions. Divide the class into groups of 2 to 5 students. Then have the students make two sets of cards the same size and color. They write the vocabulary words on one set and the definitions on the other. All cards are mixed together and placed face down on a table. A player picks two cards. If the word and the definition match, the player keeps the cards and takes another turn. If the cards don't match, they are returned face down to their places on the table, and another player takes a turn. Players must concentrate to remember the locations of the words and their definitions. The game continues until all matches have been made. This is an ideal activity for free exploration time.

- Divide the class into groups, and have them write **Group Short Stories** that include all the vocabulary words assigned. See which group makes up the shortest, funniest, or most exciting story.

- Ask your students to write paragraphs using the vocabulary words to present **History Lessons** that relate to the story's time period or historical events.

- Challenge your students to use a specific vocabulary word from the story at least **10 Times in One Day.** They must keep a record of when, how, and why the word was used.

- As a group activity, have students create an **Illustrated Dictionary** of the vocabulary words.

- Make up sentences for each word, but leave the word out. Trade papers and have a partner **Fill in the Blanks.**

- Play **Vocabulary Charades.** In this game, vocabulary words are acted out.

You probably have many more ideas to add to this list. Try them! See if experiencing vocabulary on a personal level increases your students' vocabulary interest and retention.

Quiz Time!

1. Turn this paper over and write a one-paragraph summary of the major events for each chapter in this section. Then complete the questions on this page.

2. In what trade is Johnny being trained?

   _____

   _____

3. List three reasons why Johnny is well-liked.

   _____

   _____

4. In one well-written sentence, characterize Dove.

   _____

   _____

5. Why doesn't Mr. Lapham do much silversmithing?

   _____

   _____

6. What very important customer visits Mr. Lapham's shop, and why?

   _____

   _____

7. Explain the importance of the silver cup Johnny's mother gave him.

   _____

   _____

8. Describe the accident that took place in the shop on the Sabbath.

   _____

   _____

9. Why does Mrs. Lapham send for midwife Gran Hopper instead of Dr. Warren?

   _____

   _____

10. What advice did Mr. Lapham frequently give to Johnny?

   _____

Stamp of Approval

Cilla designed a "beautiful mark" for Johnny to use when he became a master smith. She cleverly intertwined his initials J and T. But Johnny corrected her, explaining that an "L" for Lyte was needed between the J and the T.

Silversmiths usually design a stamp for their wares to identify their creations. In the 1700s, a silversmith engraved the initials of his given name and his surname on a steel die. The shaping of the letters was done while the steel was soft. The hardened steel was strong enough to withstand the repeated blows of a hammer.

Designing Your Own Monogram

If you were a silversmith, what kind of stamp would you design? For this activity you will need white scrap paper, pencils, a potato, a paring knife, printing ink or washable paint, a piece of glass about 8" x 11" (20 cm x 28 cm), a brayer, and a thick piece of paper.

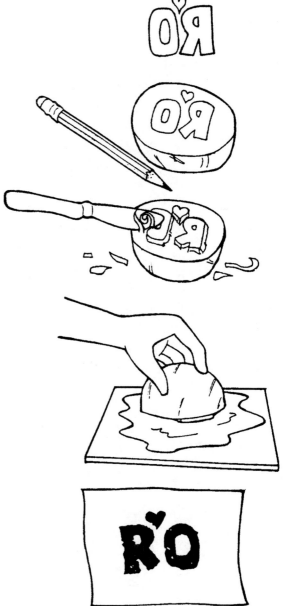

1. Practice designing your monogram on scrap paper. Try different styles and techniques for arranging your initials.

2. Choose your favorite design.

3. Slice the potato in half. Trace or sketch your initials on one of the halves.

4. Carefully carve away the parts of the potato you don't want to print by slicing down and then across with the knife.

5. Let the carved potato dry for at least an hour. This will help the ink or the paint adhere better.

6. Spread some ink or paint on the sheet of glass with the brayer. Dip the potato into the ink. Then position the potato on the thick paper (index cards, cover stock), and press down firmly. Re-ink the potato after every print or two.

Variations: Use your stamp to create bookmarks, stationery, notepaper, etc.

We Can Work It Out

A happy moment turns sour when Johnny shows up at the Laphams' with gifts for Cilla and Isannah. Cilla deeply appreciates the beautiful book and crayons and little Isannah seems thrilled to collect her limes. However, when Johnny tries to hug Isannah, she screams, "Don't touch me with that dreadful hand!"

Have you ever had your heart broken because of something that was said to you? Have you ever been involved in a situation in which someone else's feelings were crushed because of something said to them? Work in groups of three of four. As a group, brainstorm, then decide on one such situation to re-create and perform in front of the class. Perform the scene twice. The first time, act out the situation as it really happened. The second time, change the ending of the scene so that one or more characters do something to put the hurt person at ease.

Possible scenes include:

* A member of the softball team is being criticized for striking out.

* A classmate is being teased for forgetting her lunch money.

* A new student is being laughed at for getting lost on the way to the office.

There are many other possible situations. It is up to you and your group members to decide on one to perform. After each scene, take a few minutes to let the audience offer their ideas and suggestions.

First Aid

Johnny's burn was so terrible that he felt no pain in his hand at first. Then, almost at once, he passed out. Sadly, the injury to Johnny's hand was severe.

According to first-aid experts, knowing what to do for an injured person can save a life. Treating the victim correctly will help make the hospital or doctor's treatment more effective. Also, the National Safety Council states that most accidents occur in homes—not in cars, at work, or in public places.

Compare the first-aid remedies Dorcas, Madge, and Mrs. Lapham administered to Johnny with today's first-aid treatment. Find out the recommended steps to take if someone at your house gets burned. After you have finished your research and chart, share your findings with the rest of the class.

Steps taken in 1774.	Steps taken today.

Reading Response Journals

Journals invite students' active participation and help them attain a higher level of learning. They provide an opportunity for experimenting, reflecting, observing, and communicating with one's self. While reading *Johnny Tremain,* students should keep Reading Response Journals to develop both thinking and writing skills. Here are a few ideas:

- Ask students to bring in an inexpensive spiral notebook to be used for daily journal writing.

- Explain to students that the purpose of the journal is to help them pull together their thoughts and ideas as they read *Johnny Tremain.*

- Introduce each chapter by asking students to predict what will happen on the basis of the chapter's title.

- Begin the journal writing with a prompt. For example, in Section I, ask students to reflect on five things they already know about *Johnny Tremain* just by looking at the book's illustrated cover. Next, ask students to reflect on five questions they've formed about Johnny before reading the book.

- After reading each chapter, have students summarize the chapter's important events.

- Ask students to divide their journals into two columns. Instruct them to use the left column to summarize each chapter and the right column to comment on their summaries. They can comment on how they feel about Johnny, another character, or an event. The response column will give students a chance to evaluate, synthesize, analyze, and apply knowledge as it's received.

- Students can write journal entries that Johnny or Cilla might pen about themselves.

- Literary webs can be drawn in the journals. Webbing helps students understand important characteristics of story structure. To get students started, draw an unfinished web on the board or overhead.

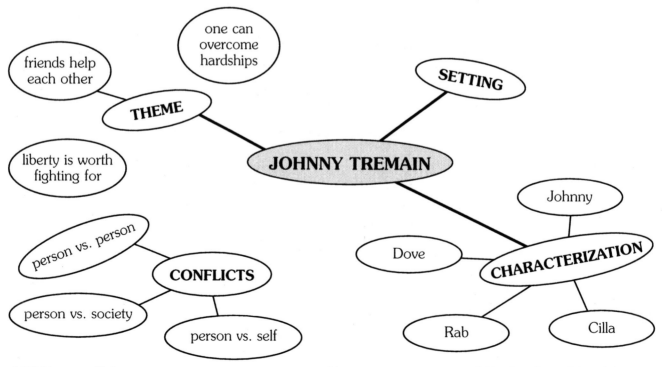

Quiz Time!

1. Turn this paper over and write a one-paragraph summary of the major events in each chapter of this section. Then complete the questions on this page.

2. How is Johnny accepted on his first visit to Merchant Lyte's?

   _____

   _____

3. Characterize Rab in one sentence.

   _____

   _____

4. Explain Rab's feelings toward Merchant Lyte.

   _____

   _____

5. What accusation does Merchant Lyte make toward Johnny?

   _____

   _____

6. List two reasons why Merchant Lyte believes Johnny is guilty.

   _____

   _____

7. What punishment does Merchant Lyte request for Johnny's crime?

   _____

   _____

8. Name the two key witnesses who testify on Johnny's behalf.

   _____

   _____

9. Why does Johnny revisit Merchant Lyte shortly after the trial?

   _____

   _____

10. What job does Johnny finally get in spite of his crippled hand?

    _____

    _____

Challenge: If you were Johnny, would you have accepted the fact that Merchant Lyte has your silver cup? Explain your answer and your reasoning on the back of this paper.

Have Your Cake and Eat It Too!

Mrs. Lorne grew very fond of Johnny. On days when he would watch the baby for her, she'd surprise him with a plate of hot gingerbread or seed cakes. In colonial America, cookbooks were scarce, and women usually traded recipes. They recorded their favorite recipes in a handmade book or on a sheet o paper. The following recipe uses the finest ingredients and makes a cake "fit for a queen."

Queen's Cake

Ingredients:

- 1 ½ cups (375 mL) raisins
- 1 cup (250 mL) butter, softened
- 1 cup (250 mL) sugar
- 5 eggs, beaten
- 1 teaspoon (5 mL) orange extract
- 2 teaspoons (10 mL) lemon extract
- 2 cups (500 mL) sifted all-purpose flour
- ½ teaspoon (2 mL) baking powder
- ½ teaspoon (2 mL) cinnamon
- extra butter to grease the baking pan
- 1 extra tablespoon (15 mL) of flour to coat the raisins

Utensils:

- large mixing bowl
- mixing spoon
- measuring cups and spoons
- waxed paper
- 9" x 5" x 3" (23cm x 13cm x 8cm) loaf pan
- toothpick

Procedure:

1. Grease the loaf pan with extra butter.

2. Preheat the oven to 350°F (180°C).

3. Spread the raisins on a sheet of waxed paper and coat them with the tablespoon (15 mL) of flour.

4. Combine the butter and sugar in a large mixing bowl.

5. Add the eggs and the orange and lemon extracts. Then add the flour, baking powder, and cinnamon.

6. Stir the raisins into the batter. Pour the batter into the loaf pan and bake for 1 hour and 20 minutes.
   (Hint: To test if the cake is done, insert a toothpick into the center of the cake. The cake is done if the toothpick comes out clean.)

7. Allow the cake to cool. Then remove it from the pan and slice.

You Be the Judge

Johnny is saved from being thrown into jail by the truthful testimony of Cilla. Then, too, Isannah's fine acting ability as she retells Cilla's story is enough to convince any judge. Only Johnny, Rab, and Cilla know she had never seen the silver cup.

How convincing can you be? Work in groups of three or four. Follow these steps and find out.

1. Listen as each member of the group shares his or her most amazing true story.

2. After hearing these accounts, select one incredible story to repeat to the class.

3. Next, make up exciting but untrue tales for each of the remaining group members. For example, in Tom, Betty, and Sue's group, Sue tells a true story of surviving an earthquake, Tom makes up a story about sleepwalking, and Betty invents an account of a UFO landing.

4. Each group gets up before the class and tells its stories.

5. As a class, vote to decide which storyteller is speaking the truth.

6. Finally, the honest group member steps forward to announce that his or her story was the truthful one.

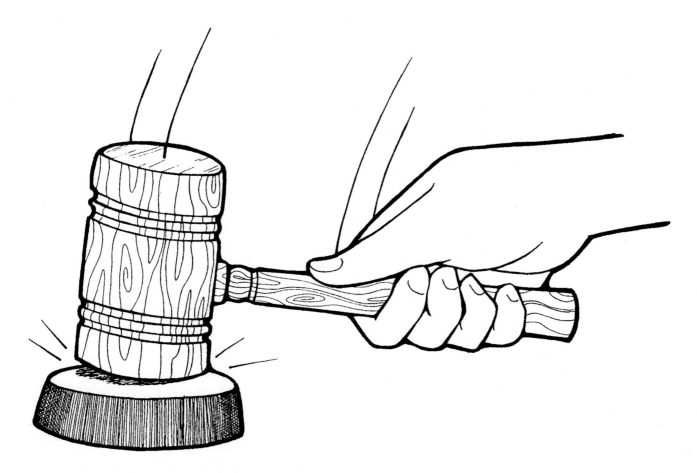

Around a Pound

Before, during, and after the Revolutionary War, the colonists used different types of money. The British pound, shilling, and pence or penny, were frequently used. Throughout the book, Johnny earns and spends pounds, shillings, and pennies. The money system was set up as follows:

Symbol	Unit	Worth
£	pound	20 shillings or 240 pence
s	shilling	1/20th of a pound or 12 pence
d	penny or pence (pl.)	1/12th of a shilling or 1/240th of a pound

Using the chart above read the problems below and calculate the answers.

1   Johnny's Income for One Week

Delivering *Boston Observer*   £2

Feeding Goblin himself   3 d.

Delivering letter to Plymouth   8 s.

Riding express for Afric Queen   4 s.

After working and saving for two weeks, what was Johnny's total?

_____

2   Johnny bought the following:

a pair of spurs   3 s.

a pair of boots   5 s.

a surtout (long overcoat)   8 s.

Calculate the total he spent in shillings.

_____

How much would this be as a fraction of a pound? (Reduce your fraction.)

_____

The value of the pound changes from day to day. Activities in money markets at home and abroad determine how much a pound is worth in American money. Suppose the British pound was equal to $1.45. To the nearest ten cents, how much was Johnny's weekly income in American money?

_____

An Heirloom, I Presume

As proof of his Lyte ancestry, Johnny's mother gave him the precious silver cup. This cup was an heirloom, a valuable possession handed down by one generation of the Lyte family to another.

What special heirloom do you or members of your family possess? Draw a picture of it in the space below and then answer the questions.

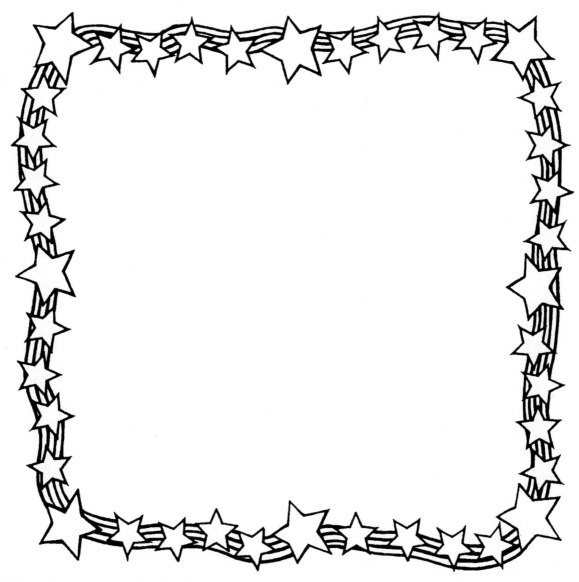

How did you come to own this keepsake?

_____

Why is it so meaningful to you?

_____

Where do you hope this heirloom will be 100 years from now?

_____

Quiz Time!

1. Turn this paper over and write a one-paragraph summary of the major events for each chapter in this section. Then complete the questions on this page.

2. Why are the colonists so opposed to the new tax on tea?

   _____

   _____

3. Explain what Johnny means when he tells certain subscribers to the *Observer*, "Eight shillings are due for your paper."

   _____

   _____

4. Where does the Observers' Club meet?

   _____

   _____

5. Identify the two leaders of the Observers' Club and list four other members.

   _____

   _____

6. Why is Paul Revere the last one Johnny tells about the upcoming meeting?

   _____

   _____

7. How did the colonists show their anger over the tea tax?

   _____

   _____

8. Why did Rab throw Dove into the harbor?

   _____

   _____

9. How did England punish the colonists for their opposition to the tea tax?

   _____

   _____

10. What effects did Britain's punishment have on the colonists?

   _____

   _____

Challenge: If you had lived in Boston at this time, would you have joined the Observers' Club? Justify your decision on the back of this paper.

Quill Skill

In Chapter 6, Johnny was told to inform John Hancock that the Observers' Club was meeting that very night. But Johnny couldn't get in to see Mr. Hancock because he was in bed with a headache. He solved the problem by writing a note and sending it to Mr. Hancock on his tea tray. What tools did young Johnny use to write with? The ballpoint pen was not available until the late 1800s. During the 1700s, quill pens were used. A quill is the hollow shaft of a bird's feather. Geese or swans provided the best quills for pens. By making your own quill pen you will discover first-hand what it was like to write with such a tool.

Materials needed:

- bird's feather (available at a craft or hobby store)
- paper towels
- sharp scissors or a penknife*
- washable ink (available at a craft or hobby store)

Procedure:

Step 1: Find a suitable feather.

Step 2: Strip off the feather from the flat end of the quill. This will allow you to hold the pen comfortably.

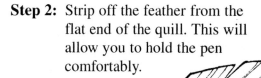

Step 3: Using scissors or a penknife, form the penpoint by cutting the fat tip at a slant, curving the cut slightly.

Step 4: Cut a small slit in the penpoint, about one-eighth inch (3.1 mm) right up the middle from the tip.

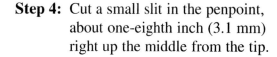

Step 5: Check the inside of the hollow quill point to be sure it's open and smooth. If the point is not open, use the end of a paper clip to clean it.

Step 6: Dip the tip of your pen into the ink. After some practice you'll get a feel for how far to dip so the ink won't blob on the paper.

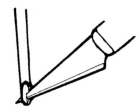

Step 7: Experiment! Hold your pen at different angles or cut a new point at a slightly different slant.

Safety Warning: Students should be careful when using a sharp object.

Masquerade Model

The patriots who took part in the Boston Tea Party disguised themselves as Native Americans. Johnny spent hours making an outfit from a red blanket that Mrs. Lorne had given him. Rab wore an old blanket coat and a "ridiculous befeathered knitted cap."

Activity:

Have groups of three or four students use scotch tape and a handful of old newspapers to create a disguise. Select one member of the group to be the model. Fold, tape, tear, and fit the paper to make a costume for the model. When designing the costume for the Boston Tea Party, use your imagination. Don't forget, your model will need some tools for breaking open the chests of tea.

After each group has finished its costume, have a fashion show. One student models the costume while the other members of the group act as announcers. Have the student announcer write a detailed description of the costume being featured. Have them consider the following in their description:

- What does the costume look like?
- Describe the color, the texture, the fit, the style.
- Who would wear this costume?
- Is it appropriate for only the Boston Tea Party?
- How does this serve as a disguise?
- Does it cover the head?
- Does it make the person wearing it easily blend into a crowd?

Use the answers to the questions to write a lively description. Rehearse it so the show goes smoothly.

Play a tape, a record, or piano music representative of America in the 1770s. "Yankee Doodle" would be a good choice.

Tea For You?

On December 16th, Johnny, Rab, Paul Revere, and many other patriots disguised themselves as Native Americans and took part in the Boston Tea Party. When Samuel Adams gave the signal, they went to work dumping hundreds of chests of tea into the Boston Harbor. It was their way of protesting the hated Tea Act. The Tea Act of 1773 put a tax on tea and gave the British East India Company a monopoly on the colonial tea trade. How much do you know about tea? Research to find answers to the questions below.

1. What two countries lead the world in the production of tea?

    _____

2. What type of plant produces tea?

    _____

3. What part of the plant is used in the production of tea?

    _____

4. What is a "tea garden?"

    _____

5. List the three different kinds of tea and explain how they are different.

    _____

    _____

    _____

6. What determines a tea's taste and flavor?

    _____

7. When and how did tea first make its way to European countries?

    _____

    _____

8. When and how was tea first introduced to the American colonies?

    _____

9. When and where was iced tea introduced to the American people?

    _____

    _____

10. Find a simple recipe for a tea-based drink. Describe it in your own words.

    _____

    _____

Some Facts About Tax

A tax is a monetary charge on a person or property that is used to pay the costs of government. In 1767 the British Parliament passed the hated Townshend Acts. The Townshend Acts taxed goods the colonists imported and used often like paper, paint, lead, glass, and tea. The colonists grew angry. They thought that a parliament by which they were not represented had no right to tax them. Their protests caused the British government to reconsider its actions. A few years later, all taxes were dropped, except the tax on tea. To protest this tax, Johnny and Rab took part in the famous Boston Tea Party.

How are you and your family affected by taxes? Do some research and complete the table below. Then answer the questions at the bottom of the page.

Type of Tax	What is Taxed	What Tax is Used For
Income		
Property		
Social Security		
Gasoline		
Sales		
Toll Road		

Questions:

1. How do you and your family benefit from taxes?

   _____

   _____

2. In what ways are taxes a problem for you or your family?

   _____

   _____

Quiz Time!

1. Turn this paper over and write a one-paragraph summary of the major events in each chapter of this section. Then complete the questions on this page.

2. Why did Merchant Lyte and his daughter return to Boston soon after visiting their country house in Milton?

   _____

   _____

3. Describe Merchant Lyte's condition.

   _____

   _____

4. Explain the significance of the Bible Johnny finds in Merchant Lyte's bedroom.

   _____

   _____

5. What is the blood relationship between Johnny and Merchant Lyte?

   _____

   _____

6. Who said, ". . . we fight, we die, for a simple thing. Only that a man can stand up"?

   _____

   _____

7. In what ways did Cilla change in two years?

   _____

   _____

8. What is the significance of Lieutenant Stranger's torn-up letters?

   _____

   _____

9. What is Dove's new job and why is Johnny working to earn his friendship?

   _____

   _____

10. Describe the trade that took place between Pumpkin and Johnny.

   _____

   _____

Tin Can Lantern

Cilla and Johnny return to the Lytes' house in Milton to try to salvage the silver. Using Doctor Warren's chaise and horse, they are able to pass through the riotous Whigs gathered in Milton. As Johnny steers the chaise onward, he stops once to light a lantern that was left in the vehicle. By its light, the two are able to assess the damage.

Materials:

tin cans washed and cleaned of all paper wrappers and glue, with the bottoms left on; various size nails; tin snips; hammer; string; coat hanger; newspaper or towels; crayons or water-based markers; sand; candle

Directions:

1. Draw a design on the can with crayon or water based marker. Do not use a permanent marker.(You do not want the design to show after creating the holes.) Design and work only on one side or area of the can at a time.

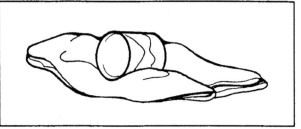

2. Fill can with sand. Put the can on a stack of newspapers or an old towel so it won't roll and to cushion the surface on which you are working.

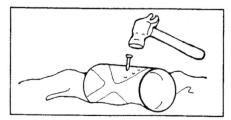

3. Use various nails to create different hole sizes. Hammer holes into the can along the design drawn. Empty sand from can.

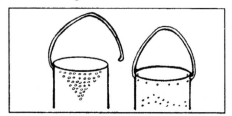

4. Use thin coat hanger wire for handles and hanging loops. Use tin snips to cut hangers. Attach the loop through design holes in the can.

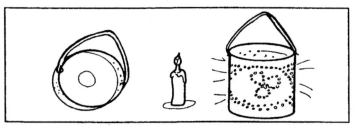

5. Attach candles to the inside of the tin can lantern by melting candle wax to the bottom of the can and placing the candle into the wax while it is still hot. The candle will adhere when the wax cools.

Note: Use extreme caution when working with tin cans as sharp edges on the top and from inside nailholes can cause injuries.

The Famous Ride

Paul Revere appears again and again in *Johnny Tremain*. Revere, the silversmith, teaches young Johnny the tricks of the trade. Revere, the patriot, attends meetings above the office of the *Boston Observer* and rides off to warn the colonists that "the British are coming." And as a friend and a concerned colonist, he joins Johnny at the Boston Tea Party.

Activity: Work in groups of three, four, or five. Have the class read "Paul Revere's Ride" by Henry Wadsworth Longfellow (pages 27-29). Discuss the meaning of the poem and compare Paul Revere in the poem to the one presented in Johnny Tremain. Also discuss the correct pronunciation of the words. Read the poem aloud several times to decide who will speak each verse. (The poem is flexible. There could be one, two, or four narrators, depending on the reading abilities of each group.) After the groups have had sufficient practice, have them take turns presenting their reading to the rest of the class.

Variations:

1. Have group members wear costumes and hats representative of colonial America. Also, one or two members of the group could hold lanterns.

2. Give groups that include reluctant readers or nonreaders a copy of Grant Wood's famous painting "Paul Revere's Ride." As the poem is presented, students can display the painting to the audience.

3. Let groups present the poem to other classes. This would be a fitting activity for April 18th—the anniversary of Revere's Ride.

Paul Revere's Ride
by Henry Wadsworth Longfellow

Listen, my children, and you shall hear
Of the midnight ride of Paul Revere,
On the eighteenth of April, in Seventy-five;
Hardly a man is now alive
Who remembers that famous day and year.
He said to his friend, "If the British march
By land or sea from the town tonight,
Hang a lantern aloft in the belfry arch
Of the North Church tower as a signal light,
One, if by land, and two, if by sea;
And I on the opposite shore will be,
Ready to ride and spread the alarm
Through every Middlesex village and farm,
For the country folk to be up and to arm."

Then he said, "Good night!" and with muffled
    oar
Silently rowed to the Charleston shore,
Just as the moon rose over the bay,
Where swinging wide at her moorings lay
The Somerset, British man-of-war;
A phantom ship, with each mast and spar
Across the moon like a prison bar,
And a huge black hulk, that was magnified
By its own reflection in the tide.

Paul Revere's Ride *(cont.)*

Meanwhile, his friend, through alley and
  street,
Wanders and watches with eager ears,
Till in the silence around him he hears
The muster of men at the barrack door,
The sound of arms, and the tramp of feet,
And the measured tread of the grenadiers,
Marching down to their boats on the shore.

Then he climbed the tower of the Old North
  Church
By the wooden stairs, with stealthy tread,
To the belfry-chamber overhead,
And startled the pigeons from their perch
On the somber rafters, that round him made
Masses and moving shapes of shade,—
By the trembling ladder, steep and tall,
To the highest window in the wall,
Where he paused to listen and look down
A moment on the roofs of the town,
And the moonlight flowing over all.

Beneath in the churchyard, lay the dead,
In their night-encampment on the hill,
Wrapped in silence so deep and still
That he could hear, like a sentinel's tread.
The watchful night-wind, as it went
Creeping along from tent to tent,
And seeming to whisper, "All is Well!"
A moment only he feels the spell
Of the lonely belfry and the dead;
For suddenly all his thoughts are bent
On a shadowy something far away,
Where the river widens to meet the bay,—
A line of black that bends and floats
On the rising tide, like a bridge of boats.

Meanwhile, impatient to mount and ride,
Booted and spurred, with a heavy stride
On the opposite shore walked Paul Revere.
Now he patted his horse's side,
Now gazed at the landscape far and near,
Then, impetuous, stamped the earth,
And turned and tightened his saddle-girth;
But mostly he watched with eager search
The belfry-tower of the Old North Church,
As it rose above the graves on the hill,
Lonely and spectral and somber and still.
And lo! as he looks, on the belfry's height
A glimmer, and then a gleam of light!
He springs to the saddle, the bridle he turns,
But lingers and gazes, till full on his sight
A second lamp in the belfry burns!
A hurry of hoofs in a village street,
A shape in the moonlight, a bulk in the dark,
And beneath, from the pebbles, in passing, a
  spark
Struck out by a steed flying fearless and
  fleet:
That was all! And yet, through the gloom and
  the light,
The fate of a nation was riding that night;
And the spark struck out by that steed, in his
  flight
Kindled the land into flame with its heat.
He has left the village and mounted the
  steep,
And beneath him, tranquil and broad and
  deep,
Is the Mystic, meeting the ocean tides;
And under the alders that skirt its edge,
Now soft on the sand, now loud on the
  ledge,
Is heard the tramp of his steed as he rides.

Pau Revere's Ride *(cont.)*

It was twelve by the village clock,
When he crossed the bridge into Medford
  town.
He heard the crowing of the cock,
And the barking of the farmer's dog,
And left the damp of the river fog,
That rises after the sun goes down.
It was one by the village clock,
When he galloped into Lexington.
He saw the gilded weathercock
Swim in the moonlight as he passed.
And the meeting-house windows, blank and
  bare,
Gaze at him with a spectral glare,
As if they already stood aghast
At the bloody work they would look upon.

It was two by the village clock,
When he came to the bridge in Concord
  town.
He heard the bleating of the flock,
And the twitter of birds among the trees,
And felt the breath of the morning breeze
Blowing over the meadows brown.
And one was safe and asleep in his bed
Who at the bridge would be first to fall,
Who that day would be lying dead,
Pierced by a British musket-ball.

You know the rest. In the books you have
  read,
How the British Regulars fired and fled,—
How the farmers gave them ball for ball,
From behind each fence and farmyard wall,
Chasing the red-coats down the lane,
Then crossing the fields to emerge again
Under the trees at the turn of the road,
And only pausing to fire and load.

So through the night rode Paul Revere;
And so through the night went his cry of
  alarm
To every Middlesex village and farm,—
A cry of defiance and not of fear,
A voice in the darkness, a knock at the door,
And a word that shall echo forevermore!
For, borne on the light-wind of the Past,
Through all our history, to the last,
In the four of darkness and peril and need,
The people will waken and listen to hear
The hurrying hoof-beats of that steed,
And the midnight message of Paul Revere.

*In this poem, Longfellow changed some of the
facts. Revere was not waiting "on the opposite
shore. " He was still in Boston when the signal
was sent. The signal was to warn friends in
Charleston to have a horse ready.*

*Nor did Revere ever get to Concord. At
Lexington, he was joined by William Dawes and
by Dr. Samuel Prescott. After the three men left
Lexington, they ran into a British patrol.*

*Revere was captured, but then let go. Dawes
escaped and got back to Lexington.*

*Prescott was the only one who managed to get
through to Concord and warn the patriots there.*

Mapping Out Revere's Ride

Johnny Tremain helps Paul Revere warn the patriots in Concord. On the evening of April 18, 1775, Paul asks Johnny to "run to Copp's Hill and tell (him) if they have moved in any of the other warships." A complete account of Paul Revere's famous ride reveals that Revere and Dawes did not make it to Concord that night. During their perilous journey, they were met by a third patriot, Dr. Prescott, who was returning home after calling on his sweetheart in Lexington. It is fortunate that he joined Revere and Billy Dawes! The three were halted by a British patrol and Revere was taken prisoner. Dawes managed to escape on foot and made his way through the woods back to Boston. But Dr. Prescott, who knew the woods even in the dark, jumped his horse and made it to Concord.

Directions: Use the map on the following page to answer questions about that famous ride.

1. In what direction is Concord from Boston?

   _____

2. What two directions did Billy Dawes travel before meeting up with Paul Revere?

   _____

3. How far is it from Lexington to Concord?

   _____

4. What separates Boston from Lexington?

   _____

5. What famous university did Bill Dawes pass on the way to Lexington?

   _____

6. According to the map, how many times did Paul Revere cross a river before reaching Lexington?

   _____

7. Which messenger traveled the longest route?

   _____

8. In your opinion, which rider faced greater dangers? Justify your choice.

   _____

9. Which is about halfway between Concord and Boston: Russell House, Hartwell Farm, or Hall House?

   _____

10. What is the importance of the "Old Boston Stone"?

   _____

11. Had Dr. Prescott failed to reach Concord, how might history have been different?

   _____

Map Of Paul Revere's Ride

Arlington to Boston: 10 miles
Lexington to Boston: 16 miles
Concord to Boston: 24 miles

Boston Stone

Old North Church

Boston Harbor

Hall House

Bunker Hill

Charlestown

Boston

Harvard College

Russell House

Arlington (Menotomy)

Buckman's Tavern

Charles River

Hartwell Farm

Lexington

Concord Bridge

Concord

Concord River

Charting Your Family Tree

After Merchant Lyte is chased out of Milton, Johnny drives Cilla back to the estate to save the silver. In the bedroom of Mr. Lyte's country home, Johnny stumbles upon a heavy Bible. Between the Old and New Testaments he finds the family's genealogy and learns that he is Merchants Lyte's grandnephew.

Genealogy gives an account of a person or a family's descent from an ancestor. You too can be a genealogist! Put your name on line 1 of the chart below. With the help of family members, fill in as much of the chart as possible. You may not be able to trace your roots back for five generations. Many years ago accurate records were not always kept. Still, it is interesting to trace your roots as far back as you can!

Complete your family tree by filling in the names of your ancestors.

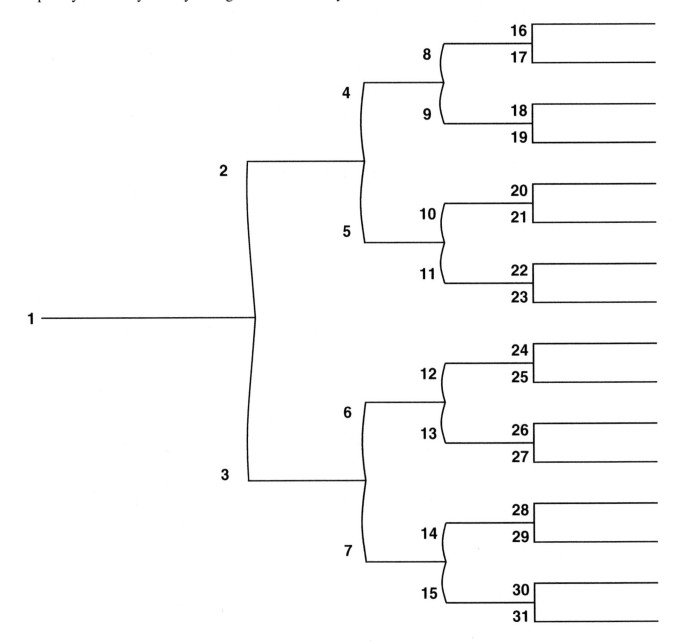

Quiz Time!

1. Turn this paper over and write a one-paragraph summary for the major events in each chapter of this section. Then complete the questions on this page.

2. Where did the war between the colonists and the British begin?

   _____

   _____

3. Explain why General Gage's orders to arrest all of the members of the Observers' Club cannot be carried out.

   _____

   _____

4. Where does Uncle Lorne hide from the British soldiers?

   _____

   _____

5. Explain the difference between Whigs and Tories.

   _____

   _____

6. What is the significance of Pumpkin's old uniform?

   _____

   _____

7. List three ways that Johnny prepared himself so that he could slip past the British soldiers and get to Charlestown.

   _____

   _____

8. What information does Johnny want to share with Doctor Warren?

   _____

   _____

9. What does Johnny learn about Rab?

   _____

   _____

10. Explain how Johnny regains the use of his burned hand.

   _____

   _____

Light the Night!

The war had begun! Word came from Lexington that the British had been "beaten by peasants." As the first day of battle came to a close, Johnny and others watched the action anxiously from Boston's Beacon Hill. Below they could see Cambridge Road filled with British soldiers retreating toward Charleston. Johnny felt the night's fresh breeze and watched as "lights began to glimmer in Charlestown and on warships."

Make your own Revolutionary light—a candle! You will need the following materials:

- Two 32-ounce (.95 L) juice cans
- Two-burner hot plate*
- Spray cooking oil
- 2 large saucepans
- Eight to ten 16-ounce (424 mL) boxes of unrefined paraffin

- Wire coat hangers *(one per student)*
- Medium-sized candlewick
- Old wax crayons *(for coloring)*
- Scissors
- Clothespin

Procedure:

1. Clean the juice cans inside and out, then spray the insides with cooking oil.

2. Place the cans in saucepans filled with 3 to 4 inches (8 cm to 10 cm) of water. Cut the paraffin into small chunks and place it in the cans. See figure 1.

3. Turn on the hot plate and heat until the water boils. Melt the wax until it fills the juice can to one inch (2.5 cm) below the rim. Continue heating by keeping the water at a low boil.

4. When the wax is melted, drop the crayons into the cans to color the wax. Use one color per pan. As the crayons melt, mix them in with the wax. Turn the burner off and allow the wax to cool slightly.

5. Dip the wicks into the wax to within an inch (2.5 cm) of the wick end. The wick may be held by a clothespin.

6. Hang the wick up until the wax hardens. When the wax is hard, dip again. This time, hold the wick over the can for a few moments. Then dip again and again. After about half an hour of repeated dipping, hang the candle up for the final drying period. (The wick can be clothespinned to a line.)

7. The wax will be firm in about an hour.

Figure 1

Safety Warning: Students should be careful when using electrical appliances or sharp objects.

Love America

Esther Forbes' novel ends with these words: "Rab had died. Hundreds would die, but not the thing they died for." The patriots believed so strongly in America's ideals that they were willing to die for them. They truly loved their country!

There are many ways to show your love for America. Work in groups of three, four, or five. List below some ways to show your love for America. For example, learn all the words to "The Star-Spangled Banner."

When you have developed your slate of ideas, share them with the rest of the class. Next, compile a class list to see how many different ways you can show your love for America! As a class project, carry out the idea—or one idea each day.

WAYS WE LOVE AMERICA

_____

_____

_____

_____

_____

_____

_____

_____

Keen Observations

When Johnny went to Silsbee's Cove looking for Grandsire, he made use of his powers of observation. He noticed that none of the pets had been fed and that the front door was unlocked. He also observed that Grandsire's old gun and powderhorn were gone. Johnny concluded that the Major had left to command his men.

It is important to develop observation skills. They will help you to think deductively and form conclusions. How sharp are your skills? Try to answer these eye-openers!

1. What president is pictured on a five dollar bill? _____

2. When Johnny's horse lies down, which end gets up first? _____

3. How many stars were on America's first flag? _____

4. What president is pictured on a dime? _____

5. How many points do the stars have on the American flag? _____

6. What does the Statue of Liberty hold in her left hand? _____

7. What is our national bird? _____

8. How many red stripes are there on the American flag? _____

9. How many stripes go completely across the American flag? _____

10. George Washington's portrait appears on the front of a dollar bill. What two symbols are printed on the back?

_____

_____

Uniforms Then and Now

For Dr. Warren's sake, Johnny had to sneak past British forces and make it to Lexington. He wore Pumpkin's old uniform so that he would blend in with the Redcoats. The shiny black hat, braided hair, and scarlet tunic made Johnny feel like a different person. All at once he felt happy, confident, and grown up.

Below are two military uniforms: one worn during the Revolutionary War and the other worn today.

1. Compare the two uniforms for comfort and usefulness.

2. Why do you think soldiers wear uniforms?

3. What uniform would you be especially proud to wear? Give the reasons for your choice.

Revolutionary War   **Present Day Military**

Any Questions?

When you finished reading *Johnny Tremain*, did you have any questions that were left unanswered? Write your questions here.

_____

_____

_____

Working alone or in groups, prepare possible answers to these questions and to those written below.

Then share your ideas with the class.

- Will Johnny enlist with the Minute Men?

- What becomes of Merchant Lyte?

- Will Cilla ever see her sister Isannah again?

- Does Isannah go on to become a famous actress?

- Will Johnny and Cilla eventually marry?

- What becomes of Merchant Lyte's property in Boston and Milton?

- How did Pumpkin get caught trying to desert?

- Does Johnny return to silversmithing?

- Did Ben Church reveal to the British secrets about his fellow Sons of Liberty?

- What kind of relationship, if any, does Johnny maintain with Dove?

- Once the war is over, what happens to the British soldiers quartered in or near Boston?

- How many lives are lost in the war?

- Does Cilla continue with her art lessons?

- What becomes of Johnny's silver mug?

- Will Sergeant Gale remain in America with Madge?

- Will Grandsire Silsbee live to see the end of the war?

- Will Mrs. Bessie work for another family after the war?

- What feelings will the citizens of Boston have for the Redcoats after the war?

- What became of the *Dartmouth,* the *Eleanor,* and the *Beaver* after their tea was dumped overboard?

Book Report Ideas

Once you have read *Johnny Tremain*, there are many ways to report on it. Choose one of the following ideas, or use your own method.

- **Radio Review**

  Write a radio script to review *Johnny Tremain*. Find fitting background music and use your "radio broadcasting" voice to tape your program.

- **Chalk Talk**

  Prepare an oral review of the book. Focus on your favorite scenes from the novel. As you tell about each scene, sketch it on the blackboard. If a blackboard is not available, use a large sheet of mural paper and markers.

- **What a Character!**

  Dress and play the role of one of the characters in *Johnny Tremain*. Visit the classroom and give a report on the book through the eyes of the character.

- **Letter It!**

  Write a letter to a family member or a friend. In your letter, summarize the novel and tell why you enjoyed reading it.

- **Game Time**

  Invent a board game using *Johnny Tremain* as the theme. Include facts and details from the book.

- **Time on the Line**

  Make a time line of the events in the story. Start with 1773 when Johnny is an apprentice for Mr. Lapham, and end it in April of 1775 with Rab's death at the Battle of Lexington.

- **Trading Cards**

  Create a trading card for each character in *Johnny Tremain*. Draw the character's face and name on the front. On the back of the card, give information about the character. You may have to make up some information, such as Dove's exact date of birth.

- **The Rap Report**

  Working alone or in a small group, write a rap song about the book. Tell what happens in *Johnny Tremain* and create a fitting beat. Perform your "rap report" in front of the class.

- **Expressive Exhibits**

  Create a diorama representing your favorite part of the book. Place it in the media center for other students to see.

- **The Ballad of *Johnny Tremain***

  Write a ballad or poem to retell the story of *Johnny Tremain*.

Research Ideas

List three things in *Johnny Tremain* that you would like to read more about.

1. _____

2. _____

3. _____

Johnny Tremain makes many references to people, places, and events in colonial history. The author, Esther Forbes, was a noted historian. By researching the topics that interest you, you will gain a better appreciation of her skillful research and writing.

In a group or on your own, research one or more of the subjects listed below. Share your findings with the class in an oral presentation.

• John Adams	• Stamp Act
• Sam Adams	• Tea Acts
• General Gage	• Yankee Doodle
• John Hancock	• Minute Men
• James Otis	• Wigs
• King George III	• Silversmithing
• Josiah Quincy	• Sailing
• Paul Revere	• Colonial Printing
• Dr. Joseph Warren	• The Boston Massacre
• Cambridge, Massachusetts	• Townshend Acts
• Battle of Lexington	• Boston Tea Party
• Battle of Bunker Hill	• "Yankee"
• Battle of Breed's Hill	• Whig Party

Back to the Future

Esther Forbes' book gives readers a glimpse of colonial Boston just before the Revolutionary War. The author spent many hours doing research. She wanted her book to depict the everyday lives of the colonists, as well as give glowing historical events.

Travel back in time to 18th-century Boston. Choose a character you'd like to portray and research his or her occupation. What tools and clothing did the work require? What conversations might have taken place? How much money could the person earn? Would he/she live in an elegant house or in a small cottage?

After you have completed your research, play the role. Be creative! Put on your costume and tell the class what you have learned from your studies. End the historical role-playing by gathering together for a sing-along. Sing songs like "Yankee Doodle" or "The Star-Spangled Banner."

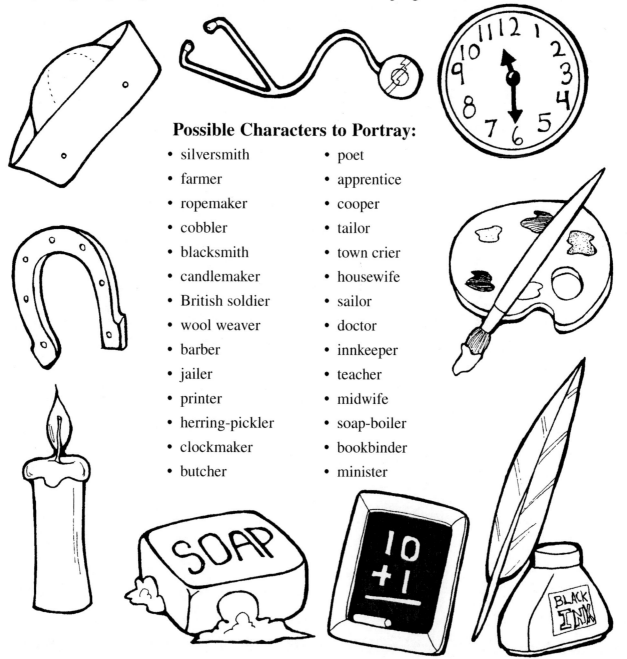

Possible Characters to Portray:

- silversmith
- farmer
- ropemaker
- cobbler
- blacksmith
- candlemaker
- British soldier
- wool weaver
- barber
- jailer
- printer
- herring-pickler
- clockmaker
- butcher

- poet
- apprentice
- cooper
- tailor
- town crier
- housewife
- sailor
- doctor
- innkeeper
- teacher
- midwife
- soap-boiler
- bookbinder
- minister

Mural Magic

Share the hightlights of *Johnny Tremain* with other students and visitors to your school. Working in groups of two or three, choose a chapter from the book. Reread the chapter and summarize it in a few paragraphs on the form below. Include the number of the chapter and the summary. Illustrate the chapter's most important event on a large sheet of mural paper. Attach the summary.

Variation: Use colorful "sidewalk chalk" to illustrate the most important scenes in the novel. Draw sketches on the playground or on an outdoor sidewalk.

Highlights from Johnny Tremain, Chapter _____

In this chapter...

_____

_____

_____

_____

_____

_____

_____

_____

_____

_____

_____

_____

_____

_____

_____

Unit Test

Matching: Match these quotes with the characters who said them.

| Lavinia Lyte | Merchant Lyte | Rab | Dove | Johnny |

_____ 1. *'There is some work here you could do .... Just riding for us—delivering papers all over Boston and around.'*

_____ 2. *'They've got maps. Maps in map cases. They've got Worcester and Concord marked in red.'*

_____ 3. *'Now, boy, you brought your cup?'*

_____ 4. *'Precious, would you rather go with me to London and be a great lady and wear silks and jewels, or stay here and be just another poor working girl?'*

_____ 5. *'I've got to go, Cil. Where's that uniform of Pumpkin's?'*

True or False:

Write true or false next to each statement below. If false, tell why.

1. _____ Mrs. Bessie is a Tory.

2. _____ The thought of going to war against the British frightens Johnny.

3. _____ Johnny's father was a French doctor.

4. _____ Isannah and Cilla remain in Boston while the Lytes return to London.

5. _____ Mr. Tweedie replaces Johnny in Mr. Lapham's shop.

Short Answer:

Provide a short answer for each of these questions.

1. What is the first battle of the Revolutionary War? _____

2. Who is Goblin? _____

3. What duty did Paul Revere and Billy Dawes carry out?_____

4. What costumes were used during the Boston Tea Party? _____

5. How many years did an apprentice serve his master to learn a trade? _____

Essay:

Answer these essay questions on the back of this paper.

1. In what ways did Johnny change during the book?

2. Throughout the novel, there are many brave characters. Who do you think was the bravest? Give reasons for your choice.

Response

Explain the meaning of each of these quotations from *Johnny Tremain*.

Chapter 1:   *'Just because some folks are not so smart, it's no reason why other folks should go around rubbing their noses in their own stupidities.'*

Chapter 2:   *Johnny did not see Dove standing on a stool, reaching far back and carefully taking out a cracked crucible.*

Chapter 3:   *Here, close to Hull Street, his mother was buried in an unmarked grave. He had not forgotten where and flung himself down beside the spot.*

Chapter 4:   *'It is perfectly obvious that this cup now stands where it belongs. The question is how was it ever separated from its fellows?'*

Chapter 5:   *This was Johnny's new life. He liked it, but was at first a little homesick for the Laphams.*

Chapter 6:   *'Look you, Johnny. I know it's Lord's Day, but there's a placard I must have printed and posted secretly tonight.'*

Chapter 7:   *But when that bill came—the fiddler's bill—that bill for the tea, it was so much heavier than anyone expected.*

Chapter 8:   *He took his knife from his pocket and cut the pages from the family Bible. Sometime they might be of use to him.*

Chapter 9:   *'They've got maps. Maps in map cases. They've got Worcester and Concord marked in red. They know where to go all right.'*

Chapter 10:   *One moment too late, Johnny ran out into the alley. He couldn't let Rab go like that.*

Chapter 11:   *The only unusual thing was the great number of feathers this deft housewife had carelessly spilled over her kitchen floor.*

Chapter 12:   *There was a sudden trickle of blood at one corner of his mouth. Rab wiped it away.*

Conversations

Work in groups to write and perform the conversations that might have occurred in each of the following situations:

- Johnny gives Cilla a writing lesson. *(2 people)*

- Mr. Lapham hears a commotion coming from his shop. He rushes out to discover Gran Hopper, Mrs. Lapham, and Cilla tending to Johnny and his badly burned hand. *(5 people)*

- Just before the Sons of Liberty meet, Paul Revere and Dr. Warren meet privately to discuss their misgivings about Doctor Church. *(2 people)*

- Several days after the Boston Tea Party Johnny confronts Dove. He questions Dove's thieving actions on board the *Dartmouth* and Dove defends himself. *(2 people)*

- Johnny visits Cilla and Mrs. Bessie at the Lyte mansion. He shows them his crippled hand which Dr. Warren has treated. Johnny also tells them of Rab's death. *(3 people)*

- Cilla visits Uncle Lorne and Aunt Jenifer at their new print shop in the quarters of the Lytes' coachman. Cilla displays her latest cartoon sketches, which she hopes Uncle Lorne can use. *(3 people)*

- Uncle Lorne and Aunt Jenifer read a letter recently sent to them by Johnny. His correspondence tells of Rab's death and his experiences as a Minute Man. *(2 people)*

- After the war has ended, Johnny petitions the court for ownership of the late Merchant Lyte's property. *(2 people or more)*

- Johnny visits Cilla's parents, Mr. and Mrs. Tweedie. He asks their permission to marry Cilla. *(3 people)*

- Paul Revere is now an old man. He tells his grandchildren of his daring ride to warn the Concord patriots back in April of 1775. *(3 people or more)*

- Madge and Cilla meet one day on the street. The war has been going on for over a year and the two sisters catch up on family news. *(2 people)*

- Billy Dawes tells his wife about the previous night's events. Billy has just returned tired and weary from his historic ride to warn the Minute Men in Concord. *(2 people)*

- From his hospital bed, Colonel Smith orders Dove to be brought to his room. Smith quizzes Dove at length to uncover any possible link between his stable boy and the British defeat at Lexington. *(2 people)*

- One day while delivering papers for *The Observer*, Johnny introduces Cilla to Paul Revere. Paul shows the two of them around his silversmith's shop. *(3 people)*

- Write and perform one of your own conversations involving the characters from *Johnny Tremain*.

Bibliography

Blos, Joan W. A. *A Gathering of Days.* (Scribner's, 1979).

Brady, Esther Wood. *Toliver's Secret.* (Crown Pub., 1976).

Brown, Drollene. *Sybil Rides for Independence.* (A. Whitman, 1985).

Caney, Steven. *Kids' America.* (Workman Pub. Co., 1978).

Chamberlain, Barbara. *Ride the West Wind.* (David Cook, 1979).

Clyne, Patricia E. *The Corduroy Road.* (Peter Smith Pub., 1984).

Collier, James L., and Christopher. *My Brother Sam Is Dead.* (Macmillan Child Group., 1984).

Davis, Burke. *Black Heroes of the American Revolution.* (Harbrace, 1976).

Flack, Jerry. "The Versatile Journal," *Writing Teacher,* Nov. 1992, pages 14-16.

Forbes, Esther. *Paul Revere and the World He Lived In.* (Houghton Mifflin, 1942).

Fritz, Jean. *The Cabin Faced West.* (Coward, McCann, 1958).

Fritz, Jean. *Early Thunder.* (Coward, McCann, 1967).

Furneaux, Rupert. *The Pictorial History of the American Revolution.* (J. G. Furguson Pub. Co., 1973).

Gauch, Patricia. *Aaron & the Green Mountain Boys.* (ShoeTree Press, 1988).

Gleiter, Jan, and Kathleen Thompson. *Molly Pitcher.* (Raintree Pubs., 1987).

Kauffman, Henry J. *The Colonial Silversmith, His Techniques and His Products.* (Galahad Books, 1967).

Lawson, Robert. *Mr. Revere & I.* (Little, 1988).

Lee, Beverly. *The Secret of Van Rink's Cellar.* (Lerner Pubns., 1979).

McDowell, Bart. *The Revolutionary War.* (National Geographic Society, 1967).

McGovern, Ann. *The Secret Soldier: The Story of Deborah Sampson.* (Scholastic Inc., 1990).

Meadowcroft, Enid L. *Silver for General Washington.* (Harper & Row, 1967).

Moore, Ruth N. *Distant Thunder.* (Herald Press, 1991).

Odell, Scott. *Sara Bishop.* (Scholastic Inc., 1988).

Reit, Seymour. *Guns for General Washington: The Impossible Journey.* (Gulliver Bks. Harbrace, 1990).

Shelley, Mary V. *Dr. Ed: The Story of General Edward Hand.* (Sutter House, 1978).

Stein, R. Conrad. *The Story of Lexington & Concord.* (Childrens, 1983).

Stevenson, Augusta. *Molly Pitcher: Young Patriot.* (Macmillan Child Group, 1986).

Strobell, Adah Parker. *"Like It Was" Bicentennial Games 'N Fun Handbook.* (Acropolic Books LTD, 1975).

Tharp, Louise H. *Tory Hole.* (DCA, 1976).

Answer Key

Page 10

1. Accept appropriate summaries.
2. A silversmith.
3. Acceptable answers include: He was clever at his work; He was reliable; He sassed and teased the girls; He was good-natured.
4. Accept appropriate characterization.
5. He was quite old and his fingers were gnarled.
6. Mr Hancock. He needed a sugar basin for his Aunt Lydia's birthday.
7. The emblem on the cup proved he was related to the wealthy Lyte family.
8. Out of spite, Dove gave Johnny a cracked crucible which when heated collapsed. Silver began spilling over the top of the furnace. As Johnny jumped toward it, he slipped on beeswax which had melted on the floor. His outstretched hand came down on top of the furnace.
9. She didn't want any doctors to know they had been breaking the Sabbath Day.
10. His advice was to be more humble and modest. Also, he advised Johnny to be more understanding of those who "weren't so smart."

Page 15

1. Accept appropriate summaries.
2. Coldly at first, but when Johnny mentioned the silver cup, Lyte became very interested in seeing him.
3. Accept appropriate characterization.
4. He does not like Mr. Lyte. He feels he is sly and crooked.
5. He accuses Johnny of having stolen the cup.
6. Last August, someone broke into Lyte's house, stealing an identical cup from his set. Mr. Lyte is also suspicious of Johnny's fine clothing. Mrs. Lapham confirms his suspicions when she swore Johnny never owned such fine clothes.
7. The death penalty.
8. Cilla and Isannah.
9. To sell him the cup—he needs the money.
10. That of a horse boy—delivering papers for *The Observer*.

Page 18

1. 5 pounds 4s 6d
2. 16s
3. ⅓ pound
4. $3.80 Explanation: 2 pounds = $2.90; 12 s = ⅗ of a pound or ⅗ of $1.45; ⅗ of $1.45 = $.87

Page 20

1. Accept appropriate summaries.
2. They refused to accept a tax unless they could vote for the men who taxed them.
3. The Boston Observers' are meeting tonight at 8:00 PM.
4. On the second story of Uncle Lorne's publishing house; in Rab and Johnny's living quarters.
5. Samuel Adams and John Hancock are the leaders. Accept appropriate responses.
6. He hopes that he will see Cilla after he visits Paul Revere.
7. They dressed like Native Americans and threw all the tea into the Boston Harbor.
8. He is loyal to England and was stealing tea.
9. They said nothing would be imported until the tea was paid for.
10. They grew angry and more rebellious. Even some Tories were angry at England.

Page 25

1. Accept appropriate responses.
2. They were attacked by a mob of Whigs.
3. Accept appropriate responses.
4. It contains the Lyte family tree—proving he is related to the Merchant Lyte.
5. He is Merchant Lyte's grandnephew.
6. James Otis
7. Possible answers include: She can now read and write. She wears fine clothes. She's become a pretty young lady. She's wiser and more confident.
8. By piecing the letters together Rab and Johnny conclude that the British were planning to attack Fort William and Mary at Portsmouth.
9. He's Colonel Smith's horse boy; Dove might accidentally share helpful information about the British forces.
10. Pumpkin trades his uniform and musket for farm clothes.

Page 30

1. west and north
2. west and north
3. 5 miles
4. Charles River
5. Harvard
6. 3
7. Dawes
8. Accept appropriate answers.
9. Russell House
10. Distances measured
11. Accept appropriate answers.

Answer Key *(cont.)*

Page 33

1. Accept appropriate summaries.
2. Lexington
3. They had all already left town.
4. In a feather bed
5. Whigs favor support for colonists' rights. Tories support British rule over the colonists.
6. Johnny uses it as a disguise to sneak into Lexington. He needs to give Dr. Warren information and he wants to find Rab.
7. Possible preparations include: had his hair braided, wore Pumpkin's uniform, rolled in muck to look like a tired foot soldier, tore his jacket, pulled a button off the jacket, stamped on his hat, rubbed mud on his face, pricked his wrist, and smeared blood on his cheek.
8. Information about the heavy number of British casualties
9. He had been fatally wounded.
10. Dr. Warren notices that Johnny's thumb is pulled out of shape by scar tissue. The doctor could cut through the scar and free Johnny's thumb.

Page 36

1. Lincoln
2. front
3. 13
4. Franklin D. Roosevelt
5. 5 points
6. a book
7. bald eagle
8. 7
9. 6
10. On the left, a pyramid with an eye at the top. On the right, the seal of the United States of America.

Page 43

Matching

1. Rab
2. Dove
3. Merchant Lyte
4. Lavinia Lyte
5. Johnny

True/False

1. false
2. true
3. true
4. false
5. true

Short Answer

1. Lexington
2. Johnny's horse
3. Warning the Minute Men of Concord that the British were planning to attack.
4. Native American.
5. seven
   Essay: Accept reasonable and appropriate answers.

Page 44

Accept all reasonable and well-supported answers.

Page 45

Perform all the conversations in class. Have students respond to the conversations in different ways as to whether they are consistent with the characters and with conversations which those characters might have.